Congressional
Research Service
Informing the legislative debate since 1914 _____

El Salvador: Background and U.S. Relations

Clare Ribando Seelke
Specialist in Latin American Affairs

June 26, 2014

Congressional Research Service

7-5700

www.crs.gov

R43616

Summary

Congress has maintained interest in El Salvador, a small Central American country that has a large percentage of its population living in the United States, since the country's civil conflict (1980-1992). Whereas in the 1980s the U.S. government spent billions of dollars supporting the Salvadoran government's efforts against the Farabundo Marti National Liberation Front (FMLN) insurgency, the United States is now working with the country's second consecutive democratically-elected FMLN Administration. Despite the potential challenges involved for both sides, analysts predict that U.S.-Salvadoran relations will remain constructive during Salvador Sánchez Cerén's presidency, as they did during Mauricio Funes' term (2009-2014).

El Salvador is facing significant economic and security challenges that the country is unlikely to be able to address without substantial external support. El Salvador posted an economic growth rate of just 1.4% in 2013, the lowest of any country in Central America. The government is running high deficits and attracting little foreign investment. Economists have cited security concerns as a barrier to investment. Although a truce between the country's gangs helped lower homicide rates in 2012 and 2013, it has unraveled and violent crime is increasing.

Inaugurated to a five-year term on June 1, 2014, President Salvador Sánchez Cerén, a former FMLN guerrilla commander, took office pledging to lead a government based on the principles of "honor, austerity, efficiency and transparency." After defeating the conservative Nationalist Republican Alliance (ARENA) candidate, Norman Quijano, by just over 6,000 votes in a runoff election held in March, President Sánchez Cerén has adopted a conciliatory attitude. Cooperation with the opposition and the private sector will likely be necessary in order for President Sánchez Cerén to address the serious challenges he inherited. Since the FMLN lacks a majority in the National Assembly, it will have to form coalitions in order to pass legislation. This could change, however, after the March 2015 legislative elections.

The direction that bilateral relations take will likely depend upon the degree to which the Sánchez Cerén government maintains security and economic cooperation with the United States under the Partnership for Growth (PFG) initiative. El Salvador is the only Latin American country that has been selected to participate in the PFG, an initiative launched in 2011 that commits both governments to work closely together in a variety of areas. Congress has provided bilateral assistance, which totaled an estimated $22.3 million in FY2014, as well as regional security assistance provided through the Central American Regional Security Initiative (CARSI) to support PFG priorities, including anti-gang and antidrug efforts. Cooperation in boosting El Salvador's competitiveness could be bolstered by a second $277 million Millennium Challenge Corporation (MCC) compact. The MCC Board has approved the agreement, but it has yet to be signed. Should President Sánchez Cerén orient his policies too much toward Venezuela or fail to combat corruption, there could be congressional opposition to funding that second compact.

In addition to security and economic cooperation, migration issues, such has how to prevent emigration by unaccompanied alien children (UAC) from El Salvador and how to reintegrate deportees from the United States into Salvadoran society, are likely to figure prominently on the bilateral agenda.

This report examines current conditions in El Salvador as well as issues in U.S.-Salvadoran relations.

Contents

Introduction

A small, densely-populated Central American country that has deep historical, familial, and economic ties to the United States; El Salvador has long been a focus of congressional interest (see **Figure 1** for a map and key data on the country).[1] After a troubled history of authoritarian rule and a brutal civil war (1980-1992), El Salvador has made strides over the past two decades in establishing a multiparty democracy. A peace accord negotiated in 1992 brought the war to an end and assimilated the leftist Farabundo Marti National Liberation Front (FMLN) guerrilla movement into the political process as a political party. In 2009, Mauricio Funes, a former journalist, took office as head of the country's first FMLN government.[2] After a razor-thin election, Salvador Sánchez Cerén, a former FMLN high commander, took office on June 1, 2014, at the helm of a government composed mainly of former guerrillas. The new government's success could hinge on its ability to work with conservative parties, the private sector, and foreign partners (including the United States) to overcome the country's challenges.

After the peace accords were signed, successive rightist Nationalist Republican Alliance (ARENA) governments in the 1990s-2000s sought to rebuild democracy and implement market-friendly economic reforms. ARENA proved to be a reliable U.S. ally and presided over a period of economic growth, but was unable to effectively address some of the country's deep-seeded problems, including inequality, violence, and corruption. Former ARENA president Francisco Flores (1999-2004) reportedly fled to Panama in 2014 after being charged with embezzling and mishandling some $15 million in donations from Taiwan that were meant for earthquake relief.[3] The Salvadoran government is seeking his extradition. Allegations of corruption have dogged former president Anthony ("Tony") Saca (2004-2009) as well.[4] Under ARENA governments, socioeconomic development advanced, but was hindered by natural disasters, including earthquakes in 2001 and several hurricanes.

Deep scars remain evident today from a war that resulted in significant human rights violations, more than 70,000 deaths, and massive emigration to the United States.[5] Old wounds could be reopened should the Salvadoran Supreme Court overturn the 1993 Amnesty Law that has shielded those who committed human rights abuses during the civil conflict from prosecution. Still, many argue that such a decision could provide justice for victims and advance human rights in the country. Some analysts maintain that the history of U.S. involvement in countering the insurgency

---

[1] For historical background on El Salvador, see: Federal Research Division, The Library of Congress, *El Salvador: A Country Study*, ed. Richard Haggerty (Washington, DC: Library of Congress, 1990).

[2] Funes' election has been described as a watershed moment in the history of El Salvador. However, an analysis of Salvadoran voting behavior since 1992 concluded that Funes' victory occurred at least partially as a result of a gradual shift leftward among Salvadoran voters that was already evident by early 2008. Dinorah Azpuru, "The Salience of Ideology: Fifteen Years of Presidential Elections in El Salvador," *Latin American Politics and Society*, Summer 2010.

[3] "Interpol Panamá Pide Enviar Solicitud Extradición de Flores, Dice El Salvador," *EFE*, May 20, 2014.

[4] After Saca's term ended, ARENA dismissed him from the party for allegedly misappropriating party funds. Although Saca's personal wealth allegedly increased dramatically while he was in office, he has never been investigated for misappropriating public funds. Gabriel Labrador, "Ganancias de las Empresas de Saca se Multiplicaron Hasta Por 16 Cuándo Fue Presidente," *El Faro*, November 19, 2013.

[5] Priscilla B. Hayner, *Unspeakable Truths: Facing the Challenge of Truth Commissions*, (New York, NY: Routledge, 2002); Diana Villiers Negroponte, *Seeking Peace in El Salvador: The Struggle to Reconstruct a Nation at the End of the Cold War* (New York, NY: Palgrave Macmillan, 2012).

in El Salvador could make relations between the United States and this current FMLN government difficult for both sides.[6]

Figure 1. Map of El Salvador and Key Data on the Country

EL SALVADOR AT A GLANCE

Population: 6.1 million (July 2014)

Land Area: 8,008 sq. mi. (about the size of Massachusetts)

Capital: San Salvador, population 1.6 million

Ethnic Groups: Mixed (86.3%), European (12.7%), Indigenous (1%)

Life Expectancy: 70.9 years for men, 77.6 years for women

Infant Mortality: 18.4 deaths per 1,000 births

Poverty: 41%

Literacy: 84.5%

Gross Domestic Product (GDP): $24.7 billion; 1.6% growth

GDP Composition by Sector: Services (60.1%), Industry (29.5%), Agriculture (10.3%)

Gross National Income (GNI) per capita: $3,590

Key Export Partners: United States (43.6%); Honduras (13.8%), and Guatemala (12.9%)

Top Exports to the United States (2013): Apparel and textiles, Electrical Machinery Parts, Sugar, Coffee

Sources: Graphic created by CRS. Map from Map Resources. Poverty figures are from the U.N. Economic Commission for Latin America and the Caribbean, GNI per capita from World Bank, and trade data are from Global Trade Atlas. Other data are from the CIA World Fact Book, May 2014.

---

[6] Héctor Silva Ávalos, "Washington y El FMLN: Aprender a Bailar," *El Faro*, March 19, 2014.

Political Conditions

Funes Government (2009-2014)

Mauricio Funes, a former journalist elected in March 2009 to lead the country's first FMLN government, remained popular throughout his term, but his Administration struggled to address many of the country's deeply entrenched economic and security problems. Funes was an independent who had periodic conflicts with members of the FMLN, including his Vice President, Salvador Sánchez Cerén. In order to secure passage of legislation, President Funes had to form coalitions with other parties, namely the populist Grand Alliance for National Unity (GANA) party formed by former President Tony Saca after he split from ARENA in 2009.

Funes has been credited with developing a variety of social programs. One of the more popular programs his government established provided uniforms and school supplies to public school students. Another, designed and overseen by then-First Lady and Minister of Social Inclusion Vanda Pignato, involved the creation of five multifaceted women's health centers throughout the country under a program known as *Ciudad Mujer*. Perhaps as a result of those efforts, some 65.9% of Salvadorans polled in May 2014 rated Funes' Administration positively even while acknowledging that security and economic conditions had worsened during his term. [7]

In the area of human rights, President Funes issued a historic apology to victims of the 1981 El Mozote massacre on the 20th anniversary of the signing of the Peace Accords. He "recognized" the Inter American Court of Human Rights ruling that El Salvador needs to reinvestigate the massacre and guarantee the rights of victims to seek reparations. He did not push for a repeal of the country's amnesty law nor urge the Salvadoran Supreme Court to extradite military officers to Spain to stand trial for their roles in the 1989 murders of Jesuit priests. [8]

While the Salvadoran public may evaluate the Funes government favorably, it has been criticized by analysts from both the right and left for failing to bolster economic growth (see "Economic and Social Conditions") below, reduce crime, or fight corruption. The Funes government expanded crime prevention programs and community policing efforts, but its security policy will likely be remembered for the way it tacitly supported and then later disavowed a truce between the country's largest gangs. Observers have criticized Funes' inability to improve transparency and accountability, particularly in the military and police. [9]

---

[7] UCA, Instituto Universitario de Opinión Pública, *Los Salvadoreños y Salvadoreñas Evalúan al Gobierno de Mauricio Funes y el Pasado Proceso Electoral*, Press Bulletin Year 28, No. 3, May 2014.

[8] In addition to the El Mozote massacre, the 1989 killing of six Jesuit priests (five Spanish citizens), their housekeeper, and her daughter at the Universidad Centroamericana (UCA) marked another of the worst instances of human rights abuses carried out by military forces during the Salvadoran civil war. In 1991, under international pressure, a colonel, two lieutenants, a sub-lieutenant, and five soldiers were tried for the Jesuit murders. Only the colonel and one of the lieutenants were convicted; a 1993 amnesty law spared them significant prison time. It has prevented other high-level former military officials from being investigated or indicted in El Salvador for their alleged roles in the massacre. A Spanish judge began investigating the massacre in 2009, however, based on the principle of universal jurisdiction for human rights abuses and the Spanish origin of five of the priests. On May 8, 2012, El Salvador's Supreme Court rejected Spain's request to have 13 former military officers allegedly involved in the murders extradited to stand trial.

[9] Daniel Valencia Caravantes and Efren Lemus, "La Idea de Crear una CICIG para El Salvador la Mató el Silencio del Presidente" *El Faro Sala Negra*, May 12, 2014.

The Funes Administration was also fraught with disputes among the Supreme Court, National Assembly, and executive branch over the separation of powers and clashes between the government and the Salvadoran private sector. Although President Funes criticized some of the court's decisions and initially challenged its authority, he did abide by its rulings, including a decision rendering his prior appointments of retired generals to lead the Ministry of Public Security and Justice and Civilian National Police (PNC), which falls under that ministry, unconstitutional. From June to August 2012, the country became embroiled in a constitutional crisis over the make-up and authority of El Salvador's Supreme Court that was only settled after a series of complicated negotiations led by President Funes himself. Nevertheless, some critics have decried Funes for causing conflict with the private sector and improperly wielding his power on behalf of the FMLN. [10]

2014 Elections: Results and Implications[11]

On February 2, 2014, El Salvador held the first round of its 2014 presidential elections. Despite a polarized electoral climate, election day proved to be relatively peaceful, albeit with low turnout of 50% (compared to 65% in the 2009 elections). Vice President Salvador Sánchez Cerén came close to winning in the first round, with 49% of the vote, 10% more than the ARENA's candidate, Norman Quijano, a two-term mayor of San Salvador. Former president Tony Saca who headed a center-right "UNIDAD" or "Unity Movement" coalition led by the GANA party he started in 2009 likely siphoned voters from Quijano by garnering 11.4% of the vote. Because no candidate won the required 50% of the votes cast, a runoff election had to be held.

The March 9, 2014 runoff election between Sánchez Cerén and Quijano proved to be much closer than expected. During the run-up to the second round of voting, ARENA worked to capture Saca voters and encourage new voters to head to the polls. ARENA promised to continue the popular social programs started under Funes, but also took advantage of media reports of protests occurring in Venezuela to warn voters of what could happen under a radical FMLN government.

El Salvador's Electoral Tribunal did not certify the final results until it and the Supreme Court had dismissed all but one of ARENA's challenges to the validity of the results on March 25, 2014. The final results showed Sánchez Cerén capturing 50.1% of the vote and Quijano receiving 49.9%. Secretary of State John Kerry congratulated Sánchez Cerén on his victory in a statement following the certification.[12] ARENA accepted the results the following day and promised to be a loyal opposition party. Sánchez Cerén's extremely narrow margin of victory revealed the country's ongoing polarization between left and right. Prior to taking office, President-elect Sánchez Cerén and Vice President Oscar Ortiz adopted a conciliatory approach toward ARENA and the private sector, convening public and private dialogues between the transition team and different sectors of Salvadoran society.

---

[10] Fundación Salavdoreña para el Desarrollo Económico y Social (FUSADES), *Quinto año de Gobierno del Presidente Funes. Apreciación General*, May 2014.

[11] Linda Garrett, *El Salvador Update, March 2014*, Center for Democracy in the Americas (CDA), April 2, 2014.

[12] U.S. Department of State, "El Salvador Presidential Elections," Press Release, March 25, 2014.

Sánchez Cerén Administration

Composition and Priorities

During the presidential campaign, Salvador Sánchez Cerén sought to broaden his appeal beyond FMLN militants by running as a "progressive" and not as a hardliner. He selected Oscar Ortiz, the popular mayor of Santa Tecla, as his Vice President and ran on a "Deepen the Change" platform. Sánchez Cerén promised to keep the social programs that have been popular during the Funes government, but did not discuss controversial policies, such as the gang truce.

President Sánchez Cerén's Cabinet includes several holdovers from the Funes government, including the Ministers of the Economy, Foreign Affairs, Public Works, and Social Inclusion. Several of those ministers have formed good working relationships with U.S. officials and have participated in the PFG and MCC compact process. The Cabinet also includes historic Fuerzas Populares de Liberación (FPL) leaders, Communist party officials, and members of Tony Saca's UNIDAD coalition, some of whom have had tense relationships with the United States. The

Sánchez Cerén Biography
Born in 1944 in rural Quezaltepeque, El Salvador to a family of humble origin, Salvador Sánchez Cerén began his career as a teacher. He later transitioned from being a teacher's union leader to serving as a guerrilla commander for the Fuerzas Populares de Liberación or FPL during the war years. He was one of several FMLN leaders to sign the Peace Accords in 1992. Sánchez Cerén later served as a legislator from 2000-2008 before becoming Funes' Vice President and Minister of Education. Sánchez Cerén is generally regarded as more of a leftist than former President Funes and maintains close ties with Venezuela and Cuba. He also has a reputation for honesty and incorruptibility.

U.S. government reportedly regards Sánchez Cerén's personal secretary, Manuel Melgar, as one of the people behind a 1985 attack on a café in San Salvador's Zona Rosa neighborhood that killed four U.S. marines.[13] Some U.S. officials may also have concerns about the decision to maintain David Múnguía Payés, the architect of the ill-fated 2012 gang truce who is under investigation for allowing arms trafficking by the military, as Minister of Defense.[14] The rest of the security cabinet is composed of FMLN politicians (Minister of Justice and Public Security Benito Lara) and/or police from the FMLN ranks (PNC director Mauricio Ramírez Landaverde).

Many U.S. observers will be closely following the way in which President Sánchez Cerén manages his country's relationships with Cuba and especially Venezuela. While Cuba and the FMLN have a long history that predates the civil war, Venezuela has more recently provided significant economic investments in the country through entities associated with ALBA (the Bolivarian Alliance for the Peoples of Our America).[15] Early in the campaign, Sánchez Cerén said that he would join ALBA if elected.[16] While El Salvador has joined Venezuela's Petrocaribe[17]

---

[13] Tim Johnson, "El Salvador's Long-ago Civil War Still Colors U.S. Relations," *McClatchy Newspapers*, March 20, 2011.

[14] "El Salvador's Defense Minister Investigated for Arms Trafficking," *Latin News Daily Report*, June 11, 2014.

[15] ALBA is a block of countries that includes Bolivia, Cuba, Ecuador, Nicaragua, and a few Caribbean countries that receive government to government financial support from Venezuela. Alba Petróleos is a partnership between the Venezuelan state-owned oil enterprise PDVSA (60%) and an association of FMLN mayors (40%). The Venezuelan state provides generous long-term financing to Alba Petróleos on oil purchases. Alba Petróleos has used this financing to create a conglomerate with business holdings across a range of sectors.

[16] Antonio Soriano, "Primer Acto de Sánchez Sería Ingresar al ALBA," *El Mundo.com*.sv, January 12, 2013.

[17] Since 2005, the Venezuelan government has been providing oil to Central American and Caribbean nations at subsidized costs. Eoin O'Cinneide, "El Salvador Joins Petrocaribe," *Upstream*, June 3, 2014.

program in order to obtain energy supplies at lower costs, it is less certain how active his government will be in ALBA and how the future of both those entities will fare given Venezuela's precarious economic situation. Some observers have alleged that members of the FMLN close to Sánchez Cerén involved in ALBA are aligned with drug traffickers and the Revolutionary Armed Forces of Colombia (FARC), but those allegations have been disputed by other analysts.[18]

During his inaugural address, President Sánchez Cerén stressed the importance of transparency, conciliation, social justice, respect for the rule of law, and ensuring citizen security.[19] He said he aimed to boost growth and address the country's fiscal crisis through infrastructure projects and reforms to improve the business climate; continue investing in education and healthcare; and personally lead a National System of Citizen Security that will combat "organized crime, drug trafficking, extortions, and all expressions of violence." He did not refer to gangs or the truce. President Sánchez Cerén stressed the importance of actively working with the United States on the Partnership for Growth and promoting trade with Latin America, Asia, and Europe as well.

Constraints Facing the new Government

President Sánchez Cerén is likely to encounter some difficulty in implementing his government's priorities due to his country's severe fiscal constraints (discussed in the "Economic and Social Conditions" section below) and his party's lack of a congressional majority. His government already appears to be experiencing the same type of opposition to its proposals to raise taxes from the private sector and conservative parties in the National Assembly that the outgoing Funes Administration encountered. Those groups support austerity rather than higher taxes.

El Salvador's legislative branch is comprised of a unicameral National Assembly whose members are elected to serve for three-year terms. The current legislature was elected in March 2012 and will serve through April 2015. It is highly fragmented, with the FMLN holding 31 seats; ARENA, 28 seats; GANA, 11 seats; and several small parties holding the remaining 14 seats. The FMLN needs coalition partners in order to pass regular legislation requiring a simple majority. It will need broader support – three-quarters of the votes – in order to take on additional foreign debt. It remains to be seen whether President Sánchez Cerén will work as closely with the populist GANA party as President Funes did given the ideological differences between the two parties.

The Supreme Court of El Salvador is comprised of 15 justices that are divided among four chambers, including a constitutional chamber. Five justices are appointed to the Court every three years by a two-thirds vote in the National Assembly to serve for nine-year terms. Following the 2009 elections, the Assembly approved five new justices after difficult negotiations. Since their installation in 2009, the five justices on the constitutional chamber of the Supreme Court have taken actions which appeared intended to check the power of the president and the legislature, something it has historically failed to do. Analysts are waiting to see whether Sánchez Cerén will be willing to abide by the Court's decisions even if they are controversial and/or difficult to implement. This could prove to be extremely challenging should the court issue rulings limiting his executive authority or overturning past legislation, such as the country's 1993 Amnesty Law.

---

[18] Elliott Abrams, "Drug Traffickers Threaten Central America's Democratic Gains," *Washington Post,* January 3, 2014; Geoff Thale, "Response to Elliott Abrams' Op-Ed in the *Washington Post*,' *Washington Post,* January 13, 2014.

[19] "Discurso de Toma de Posesión de Salvador Sánchez Cerén," *La Página,* June 1, 2014.

Economic and Social Conditions

El Salvador achieved stability and economic growth in the 1990s following its embrace of a "neo-liberal" economic model that involved cutting government spending, privatizing state-owned enterprises, and, in 2001, adopting the U.S. dollar as its national currency. As expected, dollarization led to lower interest rates, low inflation, and easier access to capital markets, but it also took away the government's ability to use monetary and exchange rate adjustments to cushion the economy from external shocks. After posting strong growth rates in the 1990s, El Salvador's more moderate growth rates in the 2000s were not high enough to improve living standards among the Salvadoran people, approximately 47% of whom continued to live in poverty in 2010 (slightly lower than in 2001).[20] Emigration reduced unemployment and infused some households with income in the form of remittances, but also caused social disruptions.

The Funes government inherited a stagnating economy attracting little foreign direct investment (FDI) and mired in debt. El Salvador's already weak economy then contracted by 3.1% in 2009, largely as a result of the impact of the global financial crisis, U.S. recession, and damage wrought by Hurricane Ida. In March 2010, President Funes and the International Monetary Fund (IMF) agreed to a $790 million package premised on the idea that as the Salvadoran economy recovered, the government would strive to improve tax administration, restrict spending, and reallocate energy subsidies.[21] The IMF agreement paved the way for more than 1 billion dollars in loans from the World Bank and Inter-American Development Bank to support anti-poverty efforts, fiscal reform programs, and the creation of an export guarantee fund. Despite support from international donors, the Salvadoran economy has continued to perform poorly due to a combination of domestic and external factors.

Growth and Investment

Rather than presiding over a period of economic recovery, GDP growth averaged just 1.7% throughout the remainder of the Funes Administration, a rate too slow to spur progress in reducing poverty and inequality. Slow growth in the United States, El Salvador's top trade partner, likely weakened U.S. demand for Salvadoran exports and limited remittance flows. In addition, a tropical storm in 2011 caused more than $800 million in damage to roads, infrastructure, and agriculture and a coffee rust outbreak in 2013/2014 reduced production in that sector, one of El Salvador's main agricultural exports, by some 60%.[22] Still, economists have identified a lack of public and private (domestic and foreign) investment in the economy as the primary reason for the country's low growth rates.[23] Over the past decade or so, FDI in El Salvador has lagged behind other Central American countries and the Dominican Republic. The IMF and others have urged the country to adopt a whole series of reforms to attract investment,

---

[20] U.N. Economic Commission for Latin America and the Caribbean (ECLAC), *Social Panorama of Latin America, 2011*, December 2011.

[21] International Monetary Fund (IMF), "Press Release 10/95: IMF Executive Board Approves US$790 Million Stand-by Arrangement for El Salvador," March 17, 2010; IMF, *El Salvador: 2010 Article IV Consultation and First Review Under the Stand-By Arrangement*, IMF Country Report No. 10/307, October 2010.

[22] Famine Early Warning Systems Network, *The Coffee Sector in El Salvador is the Most Affected by the Coffee Rust Shock in Central America*, March 2014.

[23] Economist Intelligence Unit (EIU), *Country Report: El Salvador*, May 14, 2014.

boost revenue, better target spending, and reduce the fiscal deficit.[24] The government may be able to continue issuing bonds and swapping expensive short-term debt for longer-term debt, but that is not a sustainable economic policy in the long run.

The Salvadoran government is seeking to attract foreign investment, particularly through public-private partnerships, to fund infrastructure development and is receiving U.S. support in that endeavor through the Partnership for Growth (PFG) initiative. The lack of foreign investment in El Salvador has been attributed to a number of factors, including the country's difficult business climate,[25] public security challenges, and a low-skilled labor force that is comparatively too expensive to compete with other low-cost producers. After consultations with the private sector, the Funes Administration tried to improve the country's legal and regulatory environment, combat extortion and other crimes that affect businesses, and align job training and education programs with private sector demands. A revised public-private partnerships (PPP) law that was enacted at the end of the Funes government could pave the way for President Sánchez Cerén's plans to modernize the airport, major ports, and certain highways.

Poverty

El Salvador's social challenges have been exacerbated by the country's long and violent civil conflict, persistent poverty and inequality, and family disintegration. As previously mentioned, the effects of the 2009 global financial crisis and U.S. recession set back some of the progress that had been made prior to that time in reducing poverty in the country. Nevertheless, conditional cash transfers and other social programs, largely supported by loans from multilateral development banks, helped reduce poverty between 2010 and 2013 from 47% to 41%.[26] Despite that progress, El Salvador's ranking in the U.N.'s Human Development Index (HDI) remained basically unchanged from the beginning to the end of the Funes government. El Salvador's ranking increased from 106 in 2009 to 107 in 2013. President Sánchez Cerén has stated his intention to increase social spending using revenues that should be made available by reductions in energy costs that will occur as a result of the country's recent entrance into Petrocaribe.[27]

Security and Human Rights

As with neighboring Honduras and Guatemala, El Salvador has been dealing with escalating homicides and generalized crime committed by gangs, drug traffickers, and other criminal groups. El Salvador recorded a homicide rate of 41.2 per 100,000 people in 2013, the fourth highest in the world.[28] El Salvador has the highest concentration of gang members per capita in Central America;[29] as a result, gangs, namely the Mara Salvatrucha (MS-13) and 18th Street

---

[24] IMF, *IMF Executive Board Concludes 2013 Article IV Consultation with El Salvador*, May 22, 2013.

[25] El Salvador ranked lowest among the CAFTA-DR countries in the World Bank's 2013 Ease of Doing Business rankings. The World Bank, *Doing Business*, 2013.

[26] ECLAC, *Preliminary Overview of the Economies of Latin America and the Caribbean*, February 2014.

[27] Amadeo Cabrera et al. "El Salvador Ingreso a Acuerdo Petrocaribe," *La Prensa Gráfica*, June 3, 2014.

[28] UNODC, *Global Study on Homicide 2013: Trends, Contexts, Data*, March 2014.

[29] UNODC, *Transnational Organized Crime in Central America and the Caribbean: a Threat Assessment*, September 2012. Hereinafter, UNODC, September 2012.

gang,[30] are likely responsible for a higher percentage of homicides there than in neighboring countries. Drug trafficking organizations, including Mexican groups such as Los Zetas, have increased their illicit activities in El Salvador, including money laundering, albeit to a lesser extent than in Honduras and Guatemala. Some analysts assert that connections between drug traffickers and the MS-13 gang are fairly well developed; others doubt that assertion.[31] President Sánchez Cerén mentioned the importance of combating organized crime and drug trafficking in his inaugural address, but did not refer to gangs specifically. His Minister of Justice and Public Security has since said that the government will not support a truce with the gangs, but will allow dialogue among gang leaders to continue.[32]

Amidst a climate of extreme violence and severe human rights abuses perpetrated by criminal groups, the State Department has reported that some Salvadoran military and police have been accused of involvement in unlawful killings and torture.[33] Abuses were common in the 2000s as successive ARENA government's launched aggressive "mano-dura" anti-gang policies.[34] El Salvador's Attorney General for human rights has begun investigating recent cases in which gang members may have been killed by paramilitary death squads; PNC officials have denied police involvement in those murders.[35] It will be a challenge for the Sánchez Cerén government to ensure that security officials (both police and military) do not engage in human rights abuses when carrying out law enforcement functions.

Police, Military, and Judicial Capabilities

In recent years, much has been written about the governance problems that have made El Salvador and other Central American countries susceptible to the influence of criminal elements and unable to guarantee citizen security. Resource constraints in the security sector have persisted over time as governments have failed to increase taxes. A lack of confidence in the underfunded public security forces has led many businesses and wealthy individuals in the region to turn to private security firms. As of 2013, El Salvador's Civilian National Police (PNC) had roughly 22,000 police while there were 28,600 private security guards working for firms in El Salvador.[36]

---

[30] The 18th Street gang was formed by Mexican youth in the Rampart section of Los Angeles in the 1960s who were not accepted into existing Hispanic gangs. It was the first Hispanic gang to accept members from all races and to recruit members from other states. MS-13 was created during the 1980s by Salvadorans in Los Angeles who had fled the country's civil conflict. Both gangs later expanded their operations to Central America. For background, see: CRS Report RL34112, *Gangs in Central America*, by Clare Ribando Seelke.

[31] Douglas Farah and Pamela Phillips Lum, *Central American Gangs and Transnational Criminal Organizations*, International Assessment and Strategy Center, February 2013; UNODC, September 2012.

[32] "Sánchez Cerén and the gang 'truce': redefinition," *Latin News Daily Report*, June 25, 2014.

[33] U.S. Department of State, *Country Report on Human Rights Practices: El Salvador*, February 2014.

[34] *Mano dura* approaches have typically involved incarcerating large numbers of youth (often those with visible tattoos) for illicit association, and increasing sentences for gang membership and gang-related crimes. A *Mano Dura* law passed by El Salvador's Congress in 2003 was subsequently declared unconstitutional, but was followed by a *Super Mano Dura* package of anti-gang reforms in July 2004. These reforms enhanced police power to search and arrest suspected gang members and stiffened penalties for convicted gang members, although they provided some protections for minors accused of gang-related crimes. Most youth arrested under *mano dura* provisions were subsequently released for lack of evidence that they committed any crime.

[35] James Bargent, "Has Gang Violence in El Salvador Sparked a Death Squad Revival?," *Insight Crime*, May 23, 2014.

[36] Red de Seguridad y Defensa de América Latina (RESDAL), *Índice de Seguridad Pública y Ciudadana en América Latina: El Salvador*, 2013.

Resource constraints aside, there have also been serious concerns about corruption in the police, prisons, and judicial system in El Salvador.

With more than 80% of the PNC budget devoted to salaries and benefits for current officers, there has historically been limited funding available for investing in training and equipment. According to the PNC's strategic plan for 2009-2014, the challenges it sought to overcome during the Funes government included "a lack of incentives and a career path for officers, deficient training and infrastructure, and a lack of intelligence capabilities, among others." Corruption, weak investigatory capacity, and an inability to prosecute officers accused of corruption and human rights abuses remain additional barriers to improved police performance.[37]

The PNC was restructured at least three times during the Funes Administration. The force began under the leadership of FMLN officials who prioritized crime prevention and internal reform, including an Inspector General who won praise from human rights organizations – and contempt from the Salvadoran Congress – for investigating PNC ties to organized crime.[38] Under pressure from Salvadoran society to reduce crime rates and reportedly from the U.S. government to replace then-Minister of Justice and Public Security Manuel Melgar because of concerns about his past role in the 1985 Zona Rosa killings, President Funes replaced the FMLN leadership at both the Ministry and the PNC with retired generals (David Munguía Payés and Francisco Salinas) in November 2011.[39] This angered human rights groups and the FMLN.

As Minister, David Munguía Payés removed most officers affiliated with the FMLN from leadership positions and appointed to key positions some officers who had been under investigation by the aforementioned Inspector General.[40] The arrest and hasty release of José Natividad Luna Pereira ("Chepe Luna"), a fugitive Salvadoran drug trafficker, in Honduras in August 2012 refocused scrutiny on Salvadoran police officers who had been under investigation for allegedly helping Luna evade capture in the past.[41] Munguía Payés' term will likely be remembered for his efforts to facilitate a gang truce that was criticized by some fellow officials, including El Salvador's Attorney General, and later abandoned by his successor.

In May 2013, the Salvadoran Supreme Court deemed that the reorganization of the Ministry and the PNC had violated the Peace Accords.[42] As a result, PNC leadership changed again as President Funes appointed a new Minister of Justice and Public Security and a new PNC director who were much more skeptical of the truce. Those leaders reportedly had good working relationships with their U.S. counterparts. According to the State Department, the PNC began to perform better in 2013 than it had in the recent past.[43]

---

[37] U.S. Department of State, *Country Report on Human Rights Practices: El Salvador*, February 2014; Héctor Silva Ávalos, *Infiltrados: Crónica de la Corrupción en la PNC (1992-2013)*, (San Salvador: UCA Editores, 2014).

[38] "Comisión Especial Cita a Inspectora Zaira Navas," *El Diario de Hoy*, September 21, 2010.

[39] "Presidencia Informa que Manuel Melgar Dejó Ministerio de Seguridad," *El Faro,* November 8, 2011.

[40] Ibid.

[41] Adriana Beltrán, "Release of Suspected Drug Trafficker in Honduras Raises Questions about Corruption in Honduras and El Salvador," Washington Office on Latin America (WOLA), August 10, 2012.

[42] Sonja Wolf, "Policing Crime in El Salvador," NACLA Report on the Americas, Spring 2012.

[43] U.S. Department of State, Bureau of International Narcotics and Law Enforcement Affairs, *2014 International Narcotics Control Strategy Report*, March 2014. Hereinafter: *INCSR*, March 2014.

Due to the weakness of the PNC and the severity of the security challenges the country is facing, El Salvador has deployed thousands of military troops to help the police carry out public security functions, without clearly defining when those deployments might end. As of April 2014, some 11,500 troops were involved in public security.[44] In April 2014, the Salvadoran Supreme Court upheld Funes' October 2009 decree that authorized the military to carry out police functions. Sánchez Cerén intends to keep the military engaged in public security efforts.

Few arrests carried out by PNC officials are successfully prosecuted in the Salvadoran justice system. The State Department maintains that "inefficiency, corruption, political infighting, and insufficient resources"[45] have hindered the performance of the Salvadoran judiciary. As Salvadoran police and prosecutors are often loathe to work together to build cases, few arrests lead to successful prosecutions. El Salvador's current criminal conviction rate is less than 5%. Delays in the judicial process and massive arrests carried out during prior anti-gang sweeps have resulted in severe prison overcrowding, with almost 27,000 prisoners being held in facilities designed to hold just over 8,000 inmates as of 2013. The State Department has described conditions in Salvadoran prisons and temporary holding cells as "harsh and life threatening."[46] Reducing prison overcrowding has become a key goal of U.S.-Salvadoran efforts.

Gang Truce[47]

When then-President Mauricio Funes appointed retired general Munguía Payés, as Minister of Justice and Public Security in November 2011, observers expected the minister to back a hardline approach to combating gangs. Munguía Payés did restructure the Salvadoran police and create a new elite anti-gang unit that has received U.S. training. However, he also lent government support to a former guerrilla fighter and deputy (who was his aid in the defense ministry) and a Catholic bishop who brokered a truce between the MS-13 and 18th Street gangs. In March 2012, Munguía Payés agreed to transfer high-ranking gang leaders serving time in prison to less secure prisons in order to facilitate negotiations between the gangs. Questions remain surrounding what exactly was negotiated with the gangs, when, and under what circumstances.[48] Munguía Payés denied his role in facilitating the truce until September 2012.[49]

Between the time the prison transfers took place and May 2013 (when Munguía Payés was removed from his post),[50] the Salvadoran government reported that homicide rates dramatically declined (from an average of roughly 14 per day to 5.5 per day). Gang leaders pledged not to forcibly recruit children into their ranks or perpetrate violence against women, turned in small

---

[44] "SC Provides Security Boost for Sánchez Cerén in El Salvador," *Latin News Daily Report*, April 14, 2014.

[45] U.S. Department of State, *Country Report on Human Rights Practices: El Salvador*, February 2014.

[46] Ibid.

[47] For background, see: CRS Report RL34112, *Gangs in Central America*, by Clare Ribando Seelke.

[48] "MS Tenía una Computadora Oculta en el Penal de Gotera," *El Salvador.com*, February 18, 2014; Carlos Martínez, "Los dos Versiones de Nelson Rauda Sobre la Tregua," *El Faro*, February 17, 2014.

[49] Carlos Martínez and Jose Luis Sanz, "The New Truth About the Gang Truce," *Insight Crime*, September 14, 2012.

[50] In May 2013, El Salvador's Supreme Court nullified President Funes' appointment of retired general David Munguía Payés as Minister of Justice and Public Security because it contravened the Peace Accords and a constitutional provision stipulating that public security must be led by an individual independent of the military. Munguía Payés' replacement, Ricardo Perdomo, has opposed the truce.

---

amounts of weapons, and offered to engage in broader negotiations.[51] They did not agree to give up control of over their territories or stop extortions.

While some—including the Secretary General of the Organization of American States— praised the truce,[52] others expressed skepticism, maintaining that disappearances increased and extortions continued after it took effect.[53] El Salvador's Attorney General criticized the truce. After the Funes government withdrew its support for the truce mediators and reduced communication between imprisoned gang leaders and gang members in the streets in mid-2013, the truce began to unravel.[54] While some gangs reportedly tried to remain committed to the truce process despite the government's antagonism, factions of the 18th Street gang, and perhaps others groups as well, eventually ceased to abide by its principles.[55] By April 2014, average daily murder rates had risen to some 9 murders a day; gang attacks on police also occurred.[56] Gang leaders had previously predicted that murder rates could increase to 20 or 25 per day should the truce unravel completely; those predictions were born out by late May 2014.[57]

Confronting Past Human Rights Violations

As El Salvador seeks to deal with current security challenges posed by criminal groups in a way that respects human rights and the rule of law, the country is also still grappling with how to confront abuses committed during the country's civil conflict.

Twenty years after the U.N. Commission released its report on the war in El Salvador,[58] Amnesty International issued a statement lamenting that the perpetrators of crimes identified in that report had not been brought to justice in El Salvador and that survivors had not received reparations.[59] In October 2013, then-President Funes signed a decree creating a program to provide reparations to the victims of the armed conflict. It is unclear how much funding has been budgeted for that program and how many people it has assisted thus far, but human rights groups have urged President Sánchez Cerén to continue supporting its provision of social benefits to victims and their families.[60] In his inaugural address, Sánchez Cerén pledged to do so and to help families

---

[51] WOLA, *El Salvador's Gang Truce: In Spite of Uncertainty, an Opportunity to Strengthen Prevention Efforts*, July 17, 2012; Randal C. Archibold, "Gangs' Truce Buys El Salvador a Tenuous Peace," *New York Times*, August 27, 2012.

[52] Eric Sabo, "Gang Truce Spurs Bond Rally as El Salvador's Murders Drop 70%," *Bloomberg*, July 23, 2012.

[53] Douglas Farah, *The Transformation of El Salvador's Gangs into Political Actors*, Center for Strategic & International Studies (CSIS), June 21, 2012.

[54] "Gang Violence Peaks Again in El Salvador," *Latin News Daily*, December 18, 2013.

[55] "Presidente de El Salvador Dice que "Mara 18" Rompió la Tregua entre Pandillas," *Agencia EFE*, April 26, 2014.

[56] Zlatica Hoke, "Criminal Gangs in El Salvador Return to War Path After Two-Year Truce," *Voice of America*, March 25, 2014; Grant Hurst, "Increases in Salvadoran Gang Activity and use of Automatic Firearms Raise Death, Injury, and Collateral Damage Risks," *IHS Global Insight Daily Analysis*, April 22, 2014.

[57] Carlos Martinez and José Luis Sanz, "Para que la Gente nos Crea Estamos Dispuestos a Dejar de Meter Jóvenes a la Pandilla," *El Faro*, January 27, 2014; Carlos Martinez and José Luis Sanz, "How El Salvador's Security Ministry Dismantled Truce, Unleashed Mayhem," *Insight Crime*, May 28, 2014.

[58] Belisario Betancur, Reinaldo Figueredo Planchart, and Thomas Buergenthal, *From Madness to Hope: The 12-Year War in El Salvador: Report of the Commission on the Truth for El Salvador,* United Nations, 1993.

[59] Amnesty International, "El Salvador: No Justice 20 Years on from UN Truth Commission," press release, March 15, 2013.

[60] Teresa Alvarado, "Organizaciones Piden al Presidente Electo Continuar con Reparación a Víctimas de la Guerra," *Transparencia Activa*, March 21, 2014.

who are seeking to find out what happened to their loved ones. It is unclear whether he will urge the Salvadoran Supreme Court to overturn the 1993 Amnesty Law, as domestic and international human rights groups have been urging it to do.

Although the Amnesty Law makes bringing cases against human rights abusers from the war era nearly impossible to do in El Salvador, some former Salvadoran military leaders who have resided in the United States for more than a decade have faced judicial proceedings regarding their immigration statuses.[61] In recent years, the Human Rights Violators and War Crimes Unit within the Bureau of Immigration and Customs Enforcement (ICE) of the Department of Homeland Security (DHS) has conducted investigations focused on human rights violations in El Salvador. In one case, Colonel Inocente Orlando Montano, one of the officials named by the Spanish judge as responsible for the aforementioned Jesuit murders, pled guilty to immigration fraud in September 2012; he has been sentenced to 21 months in prison and could then face extradition to Spain. ICE found that Montano had hidden his military past when applying for Temporary Protected Status (TPS) in the United States. In February 2014, a federal judge determined that a former Salvadoran Defense Minister, General José Guillermo García, can be removed (deported) based on his role in brutal human rights violations. The judge ruled that he "assisted or otherwise participated" in 11 violent incidents, including the 1980 killing of Archbishop Óscar Arnulfo Romero.[62]

U.S. Relations

Despite dire predictions to the contrary, U.S. relations with the FMLN government of Mauricio Funes (2009-2014) remained friendly, although several Members of Congress raised concerns about corruption in the country during his term.[63] In March 2011, President Obama highlighted the importance of U.S.-Salvadoran relations by selecting El Salvador as the only Central American country to be included in his tour of Latin America. During that trip, he announced that El Salvador had been chosen as one of only four countries in the world deemed eligible to participate in the Partnership for Growth (PFG) initiative, a new foreign aid approach involving close collaboration between the United States and partner countries. El Salvador also completed a $461 million Millennium Challenge Corporation (MCC) compact during Funes' term.[64]

Obama Administration officials have pledged to continue economic and security cooperation under the PFG with President Sánchez Cerén and urged him to work with all of Salvadoran society to reach its goals, but questions remain about what types of policies he will adopt.[65] The

---

[61] Julia Preston, "Salvadoran May Face Deportation for Murders," *New York Times*, February 23, 2012. ICE, "Former Salvadoran Military Officer Pleads Guilty to Concealing Information From U.S. Government," press release, September 11, 2012. For more pending cases, see: http://cja.org/article.php?list=type&type=199.

[62] Julia Preston, "Salvadoran General Accused in Killings Should Be Deported, Miami Judge Says," *New York Times*, April 11, 2014.

[63] See, for example, "Statement of Senator Patrick Leahy on Funding for a Second Millennium Challenge Compact for El Salvador," press release, September 18, 2013. Hereinafter: Leahy, 2013.

[64] Established in 2004, the Millennium Challenge Corporation (MCC) provides economic assistance through a competitive selection process to developing nations that demonstrate positive performance in three areas: ruling justly, investing in people, and fostering economic freedom.

[65] U.S. Department of State, "El Salvador Presidential Elections," press release, March 25, 2014; U.S. Embassy in El Salvador, "Discurso de la Embajadora de los Estados Unidos Mari Carmen Aponte en el Desayuno de la Cámara Americana," press release, April 24, 2014.

MCC is likely to sign a second $277 million compact with the Sánchez Cerén government once certain conditions are met.[66] Security and governance issues are also likely to figure prominently on the bilateral agenda, particularly now that violent crime is trending upward.

Congress plays a key role in appropriating bilateral and regional aid to El Salvador, overseeing implementation of the Central American Regional Security Initiative (CARSI), and consulting with the MCC on how El Salvador's second compact should proceed. Congress is likely to closely monitor how the government of Sánchez Cerén seeks to improve the investment climate in El Salvador, deal with the gang problem, and balance ties with the United States and relations with the governments of Venezuela and Cuba. Although U.S. officials have said that El Salvador's decision to join Petrocaribe would not impact bilateral relations, congressional concerns could arise should President Sánchez Cerén orient his foreign policy toward ALBA.[67]

Partnership for Growth Initiative

El Salvador is one of four countries that have been selected to participate in the Obama Administration's PFG Initiative, which seeks to foster sustained economic growth and development in top-performing low-income countries.[68] PFG involves greater collaboration between the donor and recipient countries than traditional U.S. assistance programs, but does not necessarily portend an increase in U.S. foreign aid. As a first step of implementing the PFG in El Salvador, a binational team conducted a diagnostic study, published in July 2011, which identified the two greatest constraints on growth in the country as crime and insecurity and a lack of competitiveness in the "tradables"[69] sector.[70] Those two concerns have become the focus of U.S. bilateral and regional programs in El Salvador.

On November 3, 2011, the two governments signed a 2011-2015 Joint Country Action Plan officially launching the PFG.[71] The Action Plan included detailed pledges by the U.S. and Salvadoran governments on how they intend to address the aforementioned growth constraints. Progress towards meeting each of 20 shared goals was to be mutually evaluated and then made public every six months. According to the plan, the U.S. government aims to help El Salvador address crime and insecurity by strengthening judicial sector institutions and supporting crime and violence prevention programs. The U.S. government also intends to help El Salvador improve its infrastructure (physical, human, and financial) and business climate in order to attract investment and boost competitiveness. Both governments aim to involve the private sector and other donors in the PFG. As such, former President Funes formed a Growth Council, composed of government and business officials, to improve public-private cooperation.

---

[66] Amadeo Cabrera, "FMLN Cede a Reformas Ley Lavado y Cumplir TLC," *La Prensa Gráfica*, May 22, 2014.

[67] Diana Arias, "Ingreso a Petrocaribe no Disolverá la "Relación Sólida" Entre EE.UU. y El Salvador," *La Página*, June 2, 2014.

[68] The principles behind the PFG Initiative are to (1) focus on broad-based economic growth; (2) select countries with demonstrated performance and political will; (3) use joint decision-making and prioritization of activities; (4) support catalytic policy change and institutional reform; (5) leverage U.S. government engagement for maximum impact; and (6) emphasize partnership and country ownership. The other PFG countries are Ghana, the Philippines, and Tanzania.

[69] "Tradables" refers to products that are or can be traded internationally.

[70] U.S. Department of State, *Partnership for Growth: El Salvador Constraints Analysis*, July 19, 2011.

[71] U.S. Department of State, *Partnership for Growth: El Salvador-United States Joint Country Action Plan 2011-2015*, November 2011, http://photos.state.gov/libraries/elsavador/92891/octubre2011/Joint_Country_Action_Plan.pdf.

Two years into the implementation of the Joint Country Action Plan, the U.S. and Salvadoran governments reported in November 2013 that 17 of 20 bilateral goals were "on track" to being met.[72] However, issues such as promoting the use of extraditions as a crime control mechanism, maintaining good relations with the private sector, and attracting FDI in El Salvador had fallen behind schedule. Possibly due to the elections and impending change in government, a six-month scorecard was not released in May 2014. Since the last scorecard was released (November 2013), some goals have moved forward, including efforts to promote investment by enacting a more flexible public-private partnership law, while others have experienced setbacks. It is likely that the Action Plan and its priorities will be revised with the new government. Advances from the November 2013 and previous scorecards have included:

Reducing Crime and Insecurity: 1) the enactment of a freedom of information law, the approval of an asset forfeiture law, and the preparation of a civil service law; 2) the creation of a task force to combat crimes against small businesses and a task force to combat crime on public transit; and, 3) the expansion of temporary employment, training, and job placements programs for at-risk youth and the establishment of full-time schools nationwide.

Improving Productivity: 1) the approval of legislation backed by the private sector that is aimed at making it easier to invest in El Salvador and to better regulate the free trade zones; 2) the progress made in the Comalapa airport modernization project and the National Assembly approval of measures to support its financing; 3) the provision of job training and placement assistance by both governments that has helped more than 13,000 job seekers find employment; and, 4) the provision of U.S. trade capacity building assistance to over 3,400 businesses that have created 2,500 jobs since the PFG began, many of which are export-oriented.

It may take some time to discern whether the actions taken by each of the governments to achieve an "on track" ranking actually lead to tangible results. For example, in the security realm, are business owners' perceptions of the level of extortion they have to confront each day improving? Will the rate of reported extortions eventually decrease? Or, in the economic realm, how do investors rank the business climate in El Salvador? Is it improving? Will FDI increase?

Foreign Assistance

U.S. bilateral funding to El Salvador amounted to roughly $27.6 million in FY2013. El Salvador is receiving an estimated $22.3 million in U.S. aid in FY2014. Despite the austere U.S. budget environment, the Administration requested a slight increase to $27.6 million in bilateral assistance for El Salvador for FY2015 (see **Table 1**). Most other countries in Latin America and the Caribbean are slated to receive a cut in aid. Nevertheless, El Salvador receives less bilateral aid than neighboring Honduras and Guatemala.

---

[72] U.S. Department of State, *Partnership for Growth El Salvador-United States, Six Month Scorecard: May 2013-November 2013.*

Table 1. U.S. Bilateral Assistance to the El Salvador: FY2011-FY2015

(millions of dollars)

Account	FY2011	FY2012	FY2013	FY2014 (Estimate)	FY2015 (Request)
DA	23.9	23.9	21.4	19.3	25.0
ESF	0.0	2.0	3.4	0.0	0.0
FMF	1.3	1.3	1.7	1.9	1.6
GHP	3.1	0.0	0.0	0.0	0.0
IMET	1.5	0.0	1.1	1.1	1.0
NADR	0.0	1.0	0.0	0.0	0.0
TOTAL	29.8	29.2	27.6	22.3	27.6

Sources: U.S. Department of State, *Congressional Budget Justification for Foreign Operations: FY2013-FY2015.*

Notes: GHP= Global Health Program (includes total funds provided by the U.S. Agency for International Development and the State Department); DA=Development Assistance; ESF=Economic Support Fund; FMF=Foreign Military Financing; IMET=International Military Education and Training; NADR=Non-proliferation, Antiterrorism, Demining, and Related Programs.

As previously mentioned, since FY2013, U.S. bilateral assistance to El Salvador has been realigned to focus on reducing insecurity and boosting productivity in the country.[73] As part of that effort, the U.S. Agency for International Development (USAID) is increasing funding for institutional strengthening, violence prevention, and private sector competitiveness programs for municipalities and small and medium sized enterprises. In contrast, health programs have ended and education programs have been reoriented. USAID's education programs now focus on in-school and out-of-school youth in high-crime communities, while tertiary programs aim to align post-secondary training and education programs with current workforce demands.[74]

The Central American Regional Security Initiative[75]

In addition to bilateral aid, El Salvador receives assistance under the Central America Regional Security Initiative (CARSI, formerly known as Mérida-Central America), a package of counternarcotics and anticrime assistance for the region. As currently formulated, CARSI provides equipment, training, and technical assistance to build the capacity of Central American institutions to counter criminal threats. In addition, CARSI supports community-based programs designed to address underlying economic and social conditions that leave communities vulnerable to those threats. Since FY2008, Congress has appropriated nearly $806 million for Central America through Mérida/CARSI. The Obama Administration requested an additional $130 million for CARSI in FY2015. According to the Government Accountability Office (GAO), between FY2008 and FY2012, El Salvador received some $80.8 million in CARSI assistance (16% of the funds appropriated).[76]

---

[73] U.S. Department of State, *FY2013 Congressional Budget Justification for Foreign Operations.*

[74] U.S. Department of State, *FY2015 Congressional Budget Justification for Foreign Operations.*

[75] CRS Report R41731, *Central America Regional Security Initiative: Background and Policy Issues for Congress*, by Peter J. Meyer and Clare Ribando Seelke.

[76] GAO, Central America: *U.S. Agencies Considered Various Factors in Funding Security Activities, but Need to* (continued...)

Millennium Challenge Corporation[77]

First Compact Completed

In November 2006, El Salvador signed a five-year, $461 million compact with the Millennium Challenge Corporation (MCC) to develop its northern border region, where more than 53% of the population lives in poverty. The compact included (1) a $68.5 million **productive development project** to provide technical assistance and financial services to farmers and rural businesses; (2) an $89.1 million **human development project** to strengthen education and training and improve public services in poor communities; and (3) a $268.8 million **connectivity project** to rehabilitate the Northern Transnational Highway and some secondary roads.[78] The MCC compact was designed to complement the Dominican Republic-Central America-United States Free Trade Agreement (CAFTA-DR) and regional integration efforts and was expected to benefit more than 700,000 Salvadorans. It officially ended on September 20, 2012.

U.S. and Salvadoran officials have touted the MCC compact's effects on development and investment in El Salvador's northern border region. According to MCC, the compact enabled the construction or rehabilitation of 220 kilometers (137 miles) of roads and 23 bridges, which Salvadoran officials maintain has helped that area attract $57 million in private investment.[79] The project also provided electricity to 33,000 families; connected 7,634 households to potable water sources; created 15,250 jobs; and gave supplies and technical assistance to 17,467 small-scale producers.[80] The Salvadoran government complemented MCC investments in each of the project areas, investing $70 million in road construction and rehabilitation alone.

Critics have challenged these results. Some maintain that roads constructed by the MCC are falling apart due to design problems and a lack of maintenance.[81] Others criticized the project for providing only limited opportunities for community input in the compact development process and for failing to complete the entire infrastructure that was promised to local communities.[82]

Second Compact Still Pending

On December 15, 2011, the MCC Board announced that El Salvador would be eligible to develop a proposal for a second compact, and in February 2013 MCC obligated $3 million to assist El Salvador with compact development. On September 12, 2013, the MCC Board approved a second five-year compact with El Salvador, this time for $277 million; the Salvadoran government

---

(...continued)

Assess Progress in Achieving Interagency Objectives, GAO-13-771, September 25, 2013, available at: http://gao.gov/assets/660/658145.pdf.

[77] See: CRS Report RL32427, *Millennium Challenge Corporation*, by Curt Tarnoff.

[78] The Compact also included $28 million for program administration and $6 million for monitoring and evaluation.

[79] Ambassador of El Salvador to the United States Francisco Altschul, "Salvadoran Ambassador Francisco Altschul: The Case for a new MCC Compact with El Salvador," *The Hill*, October 1, 2012.

[80] Millennium Challenge Corporation (MCC), "El Salvador: Table of Key Performance Results," November 10, 2012.

[81] Carlos Hernández, "Conductores Denuncian Deterioro de Carretera Longitudinal Norte," *La Página*, December 24, 2013.

[82] "¿Fomilenio: Misión Cumplida?" *Editorial UCA*, September 21, 2012.

committed to match that contribution with $88 million in complimentary investments.[83] Key compact projects include:

- **Investment Climate Project ($42 million MCC funds/$50 million Salvadoran funds):** seeks to help the government develop and implement regulatory improvements and to better partner with private investors to build infrastructure and provide public services

- **Human Capital Project ($100.7 million MCC funds/$15 million Salvadoran funds):** supports full-day schooling, reforms to the policies and operations that govern teacher training and student assessment, and a new Technical, Vocational Education and Training system that is aligned with labor market demands

- **Logistical Infrastructure Project ($109.6 million MCC funds/$15.7 million Salvadoran funds):** will widen the part of El Salvador's coastal highway that connects the airport and the Ports of La Unión and Acajutla and improve border crossing facilities into Honduras at El Amatillo.

Although the MCC Board approved El Salvador's second compact in September 2013, it has yet to be signed. In response to some lingering concerns expressed by Board Members, the Salvadoran government designed a Priority Action Plan that was then agreed to by both governments to be completed prior to the compact's signing. The Action Plan required the Salvadoran government to 1) appoint a director and deputy director to a newly-established financial crimes investigation unit in the police; 2) approve an asset forfeiture law; 3) approve reformed anti-money laundering legislation that meets international standards; 4) approve reforms to the country's public private partnership law to make it attractive to investors; and, 5) issue a revised decree on how corn and bean seed are procured that is consistent with CAFTA-DR. In May 2014, U.S. Ambassador to El Salvador Mari Carmen Aponte stated that additional progress needs to be made in strengthening anti-money laundering legislation and in opening up El Salvador's seed procurement process to multinational companies in order for the compact to be signed.[84] Sánchez Cerén officials maintain that those issues are being resolved.[85]

Trade and CAFTA-DR[86]

The United States is El Salvador's main trading partner, purchasing 45% of its exports and supplying close to 39% of its imports.[87] Salvadoran exports to the United States include apparel, electrical equipment, sugar and coffee; its top imports from the United States are fuel oil, heavy machinery, and electrical machinery. Other main trade partners for El Salvador include: Guatemala, Honduras, and Mexico.

From the 1980s through 2006, El Salvador benefitted from preferential trade agreements, such as the Caribbean Basin Initiative and later the Caribbean Basin Trade Partnership Act (CBTPA) of

---

[83] MCC, *Congressional Notification*, September 19, 2013.

[84] Loida Martínez Avelar, "Aún no Resuelven Trabas para Firma de FOMILENIO II," *La Prensa Gráfica*, May 21, 2014.

[85] Amadeo Cabrera, "FMLN Cede a Reformas Ley Lavado y Cumplir TLC," *La Prensa Gráfica*, May 22, 2014.

[86] For historical background, see: CRS Report R42468, *The Dominican Republic-Central America-United States Free Trade Agreement (CAFTA DR): Developments in Trade and Investment*, by J. F. Hornbeck.

[87] Trade data contained in this section are from Global Trade Atlas.

2000, which provided many of its exports, especially apparel and related items, duty-free entry into the U.S. market. As a result, the composition of Salvadoran exports to the United States has shifted from agricultural products, such as coffee and spices, to apparel and textiles.

On December 17, 2004, despite strong opposition from the FMLN, El Salvador became the first country in Central America to ratify the Dominican Republic-Central America-United States Free Trade Agreement (CAFTA-DR). El Salvador was also the first country to pass the agreement's required legislative reforms, implementing CAFTA-DR on March 1, 2006. Since that time, the volume of U.S.-Salvadoran trade has tended to follow trends in growth rates in the United States, with a variety of factors inhibiting the performance of Salvadoran exports vis-à-vis the other CAFTA-DR countries. Those factors have included a continued dependence on the highly competitive apparel trade, low levels of investment, public security problems, and broader governance concerns. As a comparison, El Salvador's exports to the United States increased from $2.0 billion in 2005 (the year before the agreement took effect there) to $2.4 billion in 2013. Nicaragua's exports increased from $1.1 billion in 2005 to $2.8 billion in 2013.

According to the July 2011 Partnership for Growth (PFG) assessment, a lack of competitiveness among firms in El Salvador that produce internationally traded goods has prevented the country from enjoying the full benefits of CAFTA-DR. The study found that El Salvador may be "missing eight percentage points of GDP compared to CAFTA colleagues" due to its productivity constraints. Low productivity may be due, in part, to the country's low level of human capital.

More recently, El Salvador and other Central American and Caribbean countries have become increasingly concerned about the potential impact of the Trans Pacific Partnership agreement (TPP) on their textile and apparel industries.[88] All things considered, tariff preferences provided through CAFTA-DR appear to be important in keeping apparel producers in those countries competitive in the U.S. market. A TPP agreement, if one is reached, has the potential to upset this situation. If apparel produced in Asian TPP countries gains duty-free access to the U.S. market, it could displace apparel manufactured with U.S. fabric in Central America, adversely affecting the textile and apparel industries in those countries and in the United States.

Counter-Narcotics Cooperation

Although El Salvador is not a producer of illicit drugs, it does serve as a transit country for narcotics, mainly cocaine and heroin, cultivated in the Andes and destined for the United States via land and sea. On September 13, 2013, President Obama included El Salvador on the annual list of countries designated as "major" drug-producing or "drug-transit" countries, for the third consecutive year.[89] A country's inclusion in the list does not mean that its antidrug efforts are inadequate. In 2013, Salvadoran officials seized 664 kilograms of cocaine and 908 kilograms of marijuana (roughly double what was seized in 2012), as well as $2.2 million in illicit cash. Still, corruption and inadequate manpower, training, and equipment continue to hinder El Salvador's antidrug efforts.[90]

---

[88] CRS Report R42772, *U.S. Textile Manufacturing and the Trans-Pacific Partnership Negotiations*, by Michaela D. Platzer.

[89] The White House, Office of the Press Secretary, "Presidential Determination on Major Illicit Drug Transit or Major Illicit Drug Producing Countries for Fiscal Year 2014," press release, September 14, 2013.

[90] *INCSR*, March 2014.

U.S. assistance focuses on improving the interdiction capabilities of Salvadoran law enforcement and military agencies, particularly the joint military-police task force that was formed in 2012. It also supports the Attorney General's National Electronic Monitoring Center. Future U.S. support is going to be geared at helping implement El Salvador's recently passed asset forfeiture legislation and bolstering anti-money laundering efforts. The Obama Administration has recently named José Adán Salazar, a hotel magnate whom the Salvadoran government has yet to accuse of drug trafficking, as a major drug kingpin subject to U.S. sanctions.[91]

Comalapa International Airport in El Salvador serves as one of two cooperative security locations (CSLs) for U.S. anti-drug forces in the hemisphere. The CSL extends the reach of detection and monitoring aircraft into the Eastern Pacific drug smuggling corridors. Although the U.S. lease on the airport is set to expire in 2015, President-elect Sánchez Cerén indicated that he could support allowing the United States to continue using Comalapa for five more years in May 2014.[92] El Salvador is also the home of the U.S.-backed International Law Enforcement Academy (ILEA), which provides police management and training to officials from across the region.

Anti-Gang Efforts, the Designation of the MS-13 as a Major Transnational Criminal Organization, and U.S. Programs

Since the mid-2000s, several U.S. agencies have been actively engaged on the law enforcement and preventive side of dealing with Central American gangs; many U.S. anti-gang efforts in Central America began in El Salvador. In 2004, the Federal Bureau of Investigation (FBI) created an MS-13 Task Force to improve information-sharing and intelligence-gathering among U.S. and Central American law enforcement officials. The FBI established a vetted Transnational Anti-Gang Unit in El Salvador in 2007. In addition to arresting suspected gang members in the United States, ICE within DHS began coordinating its U.S. anti-gang efforts with its Transnational Criminal Investigative Unit activities in El Salvador.

Since FY2008, the State Department has funded anti-gang programs in El Salvador with support from the Mérida Initiative/Central American Regional Security Initiative (CARSI) and a line item in the Foreign Operations budget designated for "Criminal Youth Gangs" for which roughly $35 million was provided between FY2008 and FY2012. A Regional Gang Advisor based in El Salvador has coordinated Central American gang programs, including model police precincts and a school-based, law enforcement-led prevention program, since January 2008. USAID conducted a comprehensive gang assessment in 2005 and has since supported a variety of prevention programs for at-risk youth (including 39 outreach centers in El Salvador), municipal crime prevention projects, and community policing efforts. USAID-El Salvador has begun a $42 million public-private partnership focused on crime prevention and $2 million in grant awards to municipalities that have designed innovative crime prevention projects.

On October 11, 2012, the Treasury Department designated the MS-13 as a significant transnational criminal organization whose assets will be targeted for economic sanctions pursuant to Executive Order (E.O.) 13581.[93] Issued in July 2011 as part of the Obama Administration's

---

[91] "Estados Unidos Designa a José Adán Salazar Como Capo de la Droga," *La Prensa Gráfica*, May 31, 2014.

[92] "Sánchez Cerén Mantendrá Base de Vigilancia Antidrogas EE.UU. en El Salvador," *EFE,* May 14, 2014.

[93] The criteria established for declaring a transnational criminal organization pursuant to Executive Order 13581 are available at: http://www.whitehouse.gov/the-press-office/2011/07/25/executive-order-blocking-property-transnational-
(continued...)

National Strategy to Combat Transnational Organized Crime, E.O. 13581 enables the Treasury Department to block the assets of members and associates of designated criminal organizations and prohibit U.S. citizens from engaging in transactions with them.[94] Salvadoran officials seemed surprised by the designation, with then-President Funes asserting that U.S. officials may be "overestimating the economic risk or financial risk resulting from the criminal actions of the MS."[95] U.S. officials have stood by the designation, asserting that it will provide law enforcement with new tools to advance domestic and international anti-gang efforts.[96] At least six individuals have been designated as subject to U.S. sanctions.

In mid-2013, USAID suspended funding that was intended to reimburse the Salvadoran government for costs of a small grants program to assist individuals affected by the global financial crisis. Following media allegations that the benefits of the program were being directed to gang members, USAID investigated and found that the government's implementing agency had failed to follow correct program procedures, including how participating communities had been selected. For that reason, USAID ended its funding for that particular component, intended to benefit six of the "violence free" municipalities, before any funding had been reimbursed to the government for program costs. The Salvadoran government continued the program using non-U.S. government funding.[97]

Migration Issues

The United States is home to more than 1.9 million Salvadoran migrants.[98] Salvadorans comprise the 2nd largest foreign-born Hispanic population in the United States (behind Mexico). In the 1980s, Salvadoran emigration was fueled by the country's civil conflict. Once that ended, family reunification, the search for economic opportunities, and periodic natural disasters fueled emigration. The movement of large numbers of poor Salvadorans to the United States has eased pressure on El Salvador's social service system and labor market while providing the country with substantial remittances that have constituted as much as 17% of the country's GDP.[99] On the other hand, emigration has arguably resulted in a "brain drain" of Salvadoran professionals, divided families, and left the economy reliant on remittances.

(...continued)

criminal-organizations. U.S. Department of Treasury, "Treasury Sanctions Latin American Criminal Organization," press release, October 11, 2012.

[94] The first four criminal organizations that received Transnational Criminal Organization (TCO) designations were: the Brother's Circle, the Camorra, Los Zetas, and the Yakuza. See: The White House, Office of the Press Secretary, Executive Order 13581--Blocking Property of Transnational Criminal Organizations," July 25, 2011.

[95] Geoffrey Ramsey, "El Salvador President: US 'Overestimating' MS-13," *InSight Crime*, October 11, 2012.

[96] Garrett, October 2012.

[97] Teresa Alvarado, "FISLD Continuará Financiando Programa PATI en Municipios Excluidos por USAID," *Transparencia Activa*, September 13, 2013.

[98] Anna Brown and Eileen Patten, *Statistical Portrait of the Foreign-Born Population in the United States, 2012*, April 2014.

[99] U.S. Department of State, *Partnership for Growth: El Salvador Constraints Analysis*, July 19, 2011.

Temporary Protected Status

Following a series of earthquakes in El Salvador in 2001 and a determination that the country was temporarily incapable of handling the return of its nationals, the U.S. government granted Temporary Protected Status (TPS)[100] to an estimated 212,000 eligible Salvadoran migrants. TPS has been extended several times, and is currently scheduled to expire in March 2015.

Removals (Deportations)

The United States first began removing (deporting) large numbers of Salvadorans, many with criminal convictions, back to the region after the passage of the Illegal Immigrant Reform and Immigrant Responsibility Act (IIRIRA) of 1996.[101] Many contend that deportees who were members of the MS-13 and 18th Street gangs "exported" a Los Angeles gang culture to Central America and recruited new members from among the local populations. Removals from El Salvador have risen since the mid-2000s, with a significant percentage of those removed both then and now possessing some sort of criminal record, although not necessarily gang-related. As a comparison, in FY2004, DHS removed 6,342 Salvadorans from the United States, 42.5% of whom had criminal records.[102] In FY2012, DHS removed some 18,677 Salvadorans, 46.2% of whom had criminal records.[103]

The United States has been working with the Salvadoran government in a joint effort to improve the removal process. In December 2009, a bi-national working group consisting of migration authorities from both countries was formed in Washington, DC. Two of the group's goals were to expedite the process in order to avoid immigrants spending unnecessary time in U.S. detention centers and to address more general concerns about the current process; it is unclear whether those goals were met. As previously mentioned, El Salvador became the first country in the world to receive more complete criminal history information on U.S. gang deportees through the FBI's Criminal History Information Program (CHIP) in May 2012.[104] ICE expanded a Criminal History Information Sharing (CHIS) program that began in Mexico to El Salvador in 2014.[105] The CHIS program provides a criminal history on those removed from the United States with felony records to Salvadoran law enforcement. Salvadoran police would then reciprocate by exchanging similar information with U.S. officials on deportees who have serious criminal records in El Salvador.

---

[100] See: CRS Report RS20844, *Temporary Protected Status: Current Immigration Policy and Issues*, by Ruth Ellen Wasem and Karma Ester.

[101] IRIRA expanded the categories of illegal immigrants subject to deportation and made it more difficult for immigrants to get relief from removal.

[102] DHS, Office of Immigration Statistics, *2004 Yearbook of Immigration Statistics*.

[103] DHS, Office of Immigration Statistics, *2012 Yearbook of Immigration Statistics*.

[104] U.S. Department of State, Embassy in San Salvador, "El Salvador Signs CHIP," May 9, 2012.

[105] U. S. Embassy in San Salvador, "U.S. and El Salvador Share Criminal and Migratory Information," press release, May 15, 2014.

Unaccompanied Alien Children[106]

Since 2011, several factors have contributed to a dramatic increase in unaccompanied alien children (UAC) immigrating from El Salvador (as well as Guatemala and Honduras) to the United States. Until recently, unaccompanied children had largely emigrated in search of opportunities (work and education) and/or to reunite with family living in the United States. Escalating crime and violence, as well as the government's inability to guarantee citizen security, have altered that tendency; 66% of the UAC from El Salvador interviewed by the U.N. High Commissioner for Refugees in 2013 had been abused or threatened by criminal actors.[107] Some minors are also reportedly emigrating in hopes of being granted asylum in the United States, or at least being temporarily released and reunited with family pending a U.S. immigration court hearing.[108] Flows of unaccompanied minors have increased even as the journey from Central America through Mexico to the United States has become more costly and more dangerous.

Addressing the root causes of why children are fleeing from El Salvador, how those children are treated once they arrive in the United States and the process by which they are repatriated – if applicable – are likely to be important issues on the bilateral migration agenda for the foreseeable future.[109] Vice President Joseph Biden focused on these topics, as well as the need to dissuade parents from sending their children illegally to the United States, at a meeting with President Sánchez Cerén and other Central American leaders held in Guatemala on June 20, 2014. Following that meeting, the Obama Administration announced the initiation of a five-year, $25 million crime and violence prevention program in El Salvador and the continuation of CARSI funding to address the root causes of migration.[110]

Neither the State Department nor USAID have funded large-scale assistance programs for repatriated Salvadorans. With State Department funding, the International Organization for Migration (IOM) implemented a two-phased small-scale program to assist in the repatriation of unaccompanied minors removed from the United State. The first phase, which was implemented in 2010, assisted in the reintegration of 52 children. The second phase, which was implemented in 2011, focused more on building Salvadoran government capacity to work with local communities and NGOs to support reintegration of unaccompanied repatriated minors rather than assisting large numbers of individuals.[111] The Obama Administration has announced its intention to provide $9.6 million to help El Salvador, Guatemala, and Honduras reintegrate repatriated migrants; the source of that funding was not specified.[112]

---

[106] For an examination of the domestic response to the increase in child migrants and U.S. immigration policy, see: CRS Report R43599, *Unaccompanied Alien Children: An Overview*, by Lisa Seghetti, Alison Siskin, and Ruth Ellen Wasem.

[107] U.N. High Commissioner for Refugees (UNHCR), *Children on the Run: Unaccompanied Children Leaving Central America and Mexico and the Need for International Protection*, May 2014.

[108] Julia Preston, "Hoping for Asylum, Migrants Strain U.S. Border," *New York Times*, April 10, 2014; Jennifer Scholtes, "CBP Chief: Policies may be Fueling Spike in Minors Crossing Border Illegally," *CQ News*, April 2, 2014.

[109] Jennifer Scholtes and Emily Ethridge, "Alone, Illegal, and Underage: the Child Migrant Crisis," *Roll Call*, May 28, 2014.

[110] The White House, Office of the Press Secretary, "Fact Sheet: Unaccompanied Children from Central America," press release, June 20, 2014.

[111] IOM. *Final Reports to the Government of the United States of America: Return and Reintegration of Unaccompanied Minors*, 2010, 2011.

[112] The White House, Office of the Press Secretary, "Fact Sheet: Unaccompanied Children from Central America," press release, June 20, 2014.

Author Contact Information

Clare Ribando Seelke
Specialist in Latin American Affairs
cseelke@crs.loc.gov, 7-5229

www.ingramcontent.com/pod-product-compliance
Lightning Source LLC
Chambersburg PA
CBHW052027280526
45793CB00005B/1158